THE SCIENCE OF
BASEBALL

By
William Anthony

KidHaven PUBLISHING

PLAY SMART

Published in 2021 by
KidHaven Publishing, an Imprint of Greenhaven Publishing, LLC
353 3rd Avenue
Suite 255
New York, NY 10010

© 2021 Booklife Publishing
This edition is published by arrangement with Booklife Publishing

Cataloging-in-Publication Data

Names: Anthony, William.
Title: The science of baseball / William Anthony.
Description: New York : KidHaven Publishing, 2021. | Series: Play
smart | Includes glossary and index.
Identifiers: ISBN 9781534535602 (pbk.) | ISBN 9781534535626
(library bound) | ISBN 9781534535619 (6 pack) | ISBN
9781534535633 (ebook)
Subjects: LCSH: Baseball--Juvenile literature. | Sports sciences--
Juvenile literature.
Classification: LCC GV867.5 A584 2021 | DDC 796.357--dc23

Printed in the United States of America

CPSIA compliance information: Batch #BS20K: For further information contact
Greenhaven Publishing LLC, New York, New York, at 1-844-317-7404.

Please visit our website, www.greenhavenpublishing.com.
For a free color catalog of all our high-quality books,
call toll free 1-844-317-7404 or fax 1-844-317-7405.

Find us on

Photo credits:

Cover – Cheryl Ann Quigley, David Lee, Hurst Photo, Dan Thornberg, xpixel, 2 - David Lee, 4 - KPG_Payless, Ljupco Smokoski, 5 - Suzanne Tucker, 6 - JoeSAPhotos, 7 - Michael Mitchell, mTaira, 8 - kai keisuke, 10 - Spectruminfo, 11 - Mark Herreid, 12 - Mike Flippo, 13 - Paul Yates, 14 - Tom Wang, 15 - Aspen Photo, 16 - Ahturner, 18 - Tiffany Bryant, 19 - Andrey Yurlov, 20 - JoeSAPhotos.

Images are courtesy of Shutterstock.com. With thanks to Getty Images, Thinkstock Photo, and iStockphoto.

All facts, statistics, web addresses, and URLs in this book were verified as valid and accurate at time of writing.
No responsibility for any changes to external websites or references can be accepted by either the author or publisher.

CONTENTS

Words that look like **this** can be found in the glossary on page 24.

BATTER UP!

Are you ready to learn all about the **forces**, angles, and shapes behind baseball? Then grab your bat and glove—your team is waiting for you!

In baseball, two teams of nine players take turns batting and fielding. The fielding team tries to get the batters out by catching a ball hit by a batter, tagging batters as they run, or pitching so well that a batter can't hit the ball.

PITCHER

FIELDER

BATTER

The batters must hit the ball and try to touch all four bases to score runs.

PITCH PERFECT

Pitchers try to throw the ball in a way that makes it hard to hit. If the batter swings and misses three times, or fails to swing at three good pitches, this is called a strikeout! Pitchers have to think about speed, spin, and **momentum**.

Bending your knees and pulling your arm back will help give you a powerful throw.

ANGLED ARM

BALL RELEASED HERE

BENT KNEES

STAND SIDEWAYS WITH YOUR NON-THROWING ARM TOWARD THE BATTER, AND BRING YOUR FRONT LEG UP AT A RIGHT ANGLE.

BRING YOUR THROWING ARM BACK BEHIND YOU, AND TAKE A BIG STEP FORWARD.

SWING YOUR THROWING ARM FORWARD IN A SEMICIRCLE, RELEASING THE BALL NEAR THE TOP OF THE CURVE FOR A FAST PITCH.

SUPER SINKERS

Rotate your arm forward and flick your fingers over the top of the ball to create topspin.

If you want to strike out your **opponent**, then you're going to have to learn how to spin the ball! A sinker is a type of pitch that uses topspin to make the ball curve down toward the ground.

Topspin creates both forward and downward forces on the ball. This is because the spin creates higher **air pressure** on top of the ball, which pushes it downward.

HIGH PRESSURE

BALL PUSHED
FORWARD

DIRECTION
OF SPIN

LOW PRESSURE

SINKERS CREATE HIGH PRESSURE
ABOVE THE BALL AND LOW PRESSURE
BELOW IT.

Sinkers are used to confuse the batter and make them swing above the ball.

CONFUSING CURVEBALLS

Flick your fingers around the side of the ball when you release it.

SEAM

THUMB

MIDDLE FINGER

One of the most difficult pitches for a batter to hit is a curveball. This throw puts spin on the ball to make it curve to the left or the right. To throw a curveball, place your thumb along one seam and then place your middle finger along the opposite seam.

Curveballs create low pressure on one side of the ball and high pressure on the other. If the ball is spinning to the left when it is thrown straight, there will be low pressure on the left side of the ball, making it curve to the left.

If you spin the ball to the right, it will curve that way instead.

BATTING BASICS

When it's your turn to bat, there are some important things to get right before you can hit the ball far. The way you stand will help you put lots of power into your swing.

BRINGING YOUR ARMS AND BAT BEHIND YOUR BODY GETS YOU READY TO CREATE LOTS OF MOMENTUM IN YOUR SWING.

BENDING YOUR KNEES WILL STORE LOTS OF POTENTIAL ENERGY.

EYES ON
THE BALL

A BIG SWING
WILL BUILD MORE
MOMENTUM, WHICH
WILL RESULT IN A
BIGGER HIT.

A SMALLER SWING WILL
HAVE LESS MOMENTUM,
RESULTING IN A SMALLER,
LESS POWERFUL HIT.

KNEES
BENT

As the ball comes toward you, twist your arms and body toward it while extending your knees. This transfers all of the potential energy stored in your body into your hit.

HITTING HOME RUNS

A home run is when the batter hits the ball so hard that it travels over the fence at the back of the field. When they do this, they automatically score one run for their team, or more if other batters have already made it onto a base.

SWEET SPOT ⟶

Hitting the ball with the bat's sweet spot will help you hit home runs.

When you swing, lots of energy and momentum are built up in your bat. When you hit the ball, this energy is used to change the direction the ball is moving in and to help push the ball forward. The bat's sweet spot is where the most amount of energy can be transferred **efficiently**.

ENERGY FROM SWING AND THROW TRANSFERRED TO HIT

MOMENTUM FROM SWING

BALL TRAVELING IN DIRECTION OF THROW

TERRIFIC TIMING

On the field, the batter must hit the ball within a large marked area. If they hit the ball outside of this area, the hit is called a foul and it doesn't count. Timing is crucial if you want to take the perfect swing!

THE BATTER RUNS IN A SQUARE SHAPE AROUND THE BASES TO SCORE A RUN.

Players must hit the ball within this right angle.

IF A RIGHT-HANDED BATTER SWINGS TOO EARLY, THE ANGLE OF THEIR BAT WILL SEND THE BALL OUTSIDE THE FOUL LINE.

IF THEY SWING TOO LATE, THE SAME THING WILL HAPPEN ON THE OTHER SIDE!

IF THEY SWING AT THE RIGHT TIME, THEY'LL HIT THE BALL INSIDE THE AREA, AND THEN IT'S TIME TO RUN TO FIRST BASE!

THE CAREFUL CATCH

STAND IN A TRIANGLE POSITION AND BEND YOUR KNEES TO STORE POTENTIAL ENERGY.

EYES ON THE BALL

SHOULDERS FACING FORWARD

BENT KNEES

If the ball is hit high into the air, you should try to catch it. This will get the batter out. Even after the ball has hit the ground, catching it is still important. There's lots of science that can help you make the perfect catch.

EYES ON
THE BALL

AS YOU TRY TO
CATCH THE BALL,
SLIGHTLY BEND
YOUR KNEES.

MAKE A
TRIANGLE
SHAPE

Make a triangle shape with your hands. Open your glove
for the ball to land in, and place your other hand at
an angle to trap it. Be ready to bend your arms when
catching to take some of the **impact** of the ball.

PERFECT POSITIONING

HE IS RIGHT-HANDED.

HE HASN'T HIT THE BALL WITH THE BAT'S SWEET SPOT.

THE SWING WAS QUITE AN EARLY SWING.

HE HAS EXTENDED ONE OF HIS BENT KNEES.

The next batter is up and is waiting for a pitch. As the ball comes toward him, he swings to hit it, and you've got to be in the right place to catch it.

Look at both of these images. If you were a fielder and you saw the batter making this swing, in which area of the field would you want to be?

SPOT THE BALL

That's right! It's number 3! Let's take a closer look at the science behind the hit.

PLACEMENT

The batter didn't hit the ball with the sweet spot on the bat. This means the energy **dispersed** into the bat rather than the ball, so the ball didn't travel very far. Positions 1 and 2 would have been too far away!

FORCES

The batter has extended one of his knees, turning potential energy into movement energy. This will help the ball travel farther to the left-hand side of the field.

ANGLES

The timing of the batter's swing was early. This means he hit the ball when he was almost finished swinging, sending the ball off to the left! Running to spot 2 or 4 would be a waste of energy!

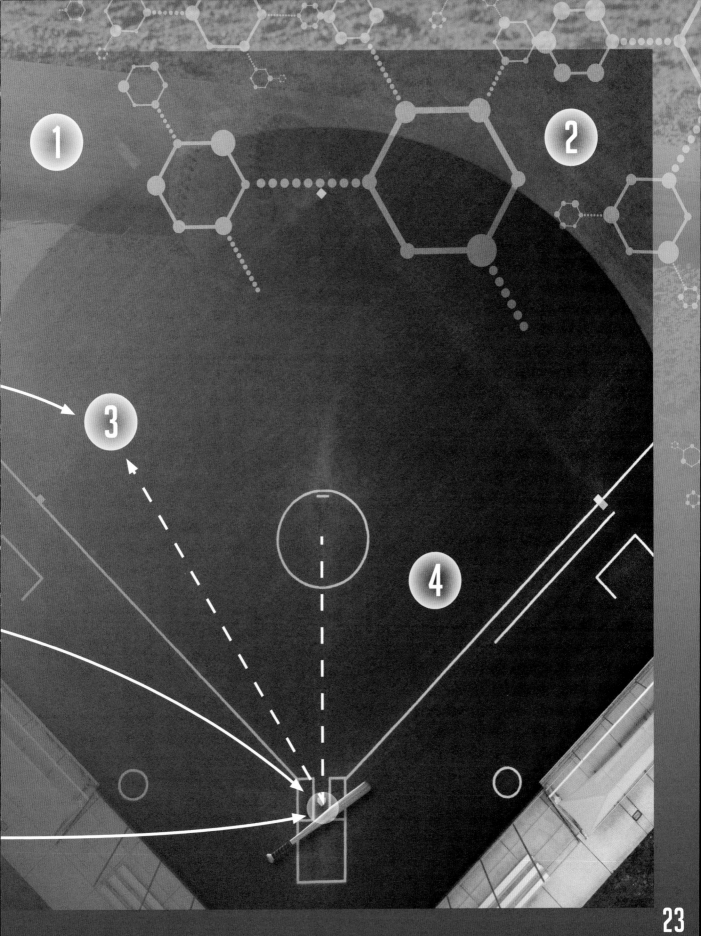

GLOSSARY

air pressure	the force the air exerts on any surface in contact with it
dispersed	spread out
efficiently	getting the most out of something in the best way possible
forces	pushes or pulls on an object
impact	the act or force of one thing hitting another
momentum	the force an object has when it is moving, based on its speed and weight
opponent	a member of the team playing against you
potential energy	the amount of energy stored inside an object that is ready to be used

INDEX